YVONNE MATZK

CONDITIONING KILLS CONFIDENCE

Some of the characters in this book are fictitious, invented to represent the traits and characteristics of people I have encountered or witnessed throughout my own personal journey.

Book Cover by Yvonne Matzk

Illustrations by Yvonne Matzk

Produced and published by Coachere Ltd

First edition 2023

To my daughter Alexia, who inspires me and motivates me every day. Courageous, compassionate, confident, kind and a little bit crazy, do not ever change.

To my husband Rob, both my harshest critic and biggest fan in equal measure. Thank you for your unwavering support and belief in me.

Note to Reader

I am a straight white woman, living in the UK and I am writing this from my own personal experiences, what I have witnessed and researched. Therefore, experiences are likely to be different for men, people of colour, LGBTQ+, people with a disability and those from different cultures.

Please also note that some of the characters in the book are not real, they are fictious characters, invented to represent the traits and individuals I have encountered or witnessed throughout my own personal journey.

It is also not the intention to demonise any of these characters or traits, I simply intend to highlight how they could be holding you back from greater confidence or self-belief.

This book has been designed, to make it easy to keep it to hand, allowing you to refer to at any point.

Contents

Yvonne Matzk

CONDITIONING KILLS CONFIDENCE

A simple, pragmatic, and honest appraisal of how the conditioning of your past may have impacted your confidence.

Background

I grew up a happy, fearless, and confident little girl who believed she could do anything because nobody told me I couldn't.

There were never any expectations put on me. I could play with whoever I wanted: girls, boys, older kids, younger kids, and kids from any ethnic background or social demographic. I always believed we were equals.

I was born in a council house and was classified as working class. Still, no social pressures were placed upon me, and my parents worked incredibly hard. The youngest of three children by eight years, I was on my own often, making me fiercely independent.

I was allowed to play out in the street or "over the green next to the river" with friends from a young age. As I was on my own a lot, I often got bored. A tennis club was at the end of the road, so I wanted to learn how to play tennis. Unbeknownst to my parents, I took myself off to the tennis club, aged six and put my name down on the waiting list.

The following year, we received a letter saying I had gained a place at the tennis club and was welcome to join. My parents scraped enough money together for the membership, so I joined the tennis club.

I turned up on the first day in a Tom and Jerry t-shirt, blue shorts, black school plimsols and my mum's old tennis racket, which was nearly as big as me. Even though I was only six, I remember that day so vividly. I was so excited about having a hobby and learning to play tennis. They turned me away for not wearing the right clothes. I was distraught. That was the first time I felt different, embarrassed, and disappointed.

The tennis club had a rule that you must only wear white clothes, and my mum couldn't have seen that part of the membership letter. Seeing how upset I was and knowing how much I wanted to play, we went to the market the following week, and she bought me a white t-shirt, shorts, and some white plimsolls. I still didn't have the right size racket, but I didn't care; I would play tennis.

The following Saturday arrived, and I was so excited. Dressed in the appropriate clothing, they let me join the rest of the children for lessons.

However, I noticed something very different about the children at the tennis club. They were all immaculately turned out, spoke differently, and had tennis rackets suitable for their size. At that point, I was surprised that all their clothes carried designer labels, and their tennis rackets were at the top of the range. I was unaware of what a designer label was and what brands of tennis rackets even existed. All I knew was that I was different, spoke differently, looked different, and felt different; they all knew it too.

Had I been terrible, this may not have been an issue, but even with my oversized, ancient tennis racket and the fact that I couldn't see over the net because I was so tiny, I was good. I took to tennis like a duck to water and found something I truly loved. Tennis became my first passion, and I put my heart and soul into getting better.

However, as much as I tried to fit in, and the better I became at tennis, the more different I was made to feel. The girls were not too bad, but the boys became nasty and spiteful, often saying hurtful things or teasing me, and I couldn't figure out why. The bullying worsened when I came to the top of the league tables or won the club tournament.

They would always cheer for my opponent, which used to make me feel sad. The more they bullied me, the more it drove me to keep improving to gain acceptance. I hadn't realised then that the better I got, the worse they got. I even felt animosity from the Coach when I used to beat his niece in a match. It was coming at me from all directions.

This was the first time I experienced bullying, but it continued throughout my childhood, adolescence, and career. There was a consistent theme building.

Someone was always waiting to bash me down whenever I achieved something remarkable. Boys, girls, men and women, students, teachers, peers, and co-workers.

Every time this happened, it would dent my confidence. I would lay low for a while, withdraw into myself, and reflect on what I could have done to make them behave like that. Thankfully, it was never too long before I would dust myself off, get back up, regain my confidence, and go again.

I could never understand why this kept happening. I had only ever been friendly and kind to these people, doing my best to fit in, trying to make the square peg fit in the round hole. This went on for years, throughout my entire life, until a couple of years ago, through a recommendation from a friend, I read a book called Untamed by Glennon Doyle.

It was reading this book that highlighted the reason why this continued to happen to me.

In her book, Glennon talks about a time when she was at one of her daughter's soccer games, and a girl on the other team was rubbing her up the wrong way. By the side-line body language and eye-rolling, she could tell she was also rubbing several of her soccer mum friends the wrong way.

Glennon observed her, trying to figure out why this girl was activating them, as she walked with her head held high and with a bit of a swagger. She was good, and she knew it. She went in for the ball often and hard like a girl who knows her strength and talent, and she smiled the whole time like all of it was easy for her. She was having the time of her life, which annoyed Glennon. She was 12.

Glennon sat with her feelings and then realised her knee-jerk reaction to this girl directly resulted from her training. She had been conditioned to mistrust and dislike strong, confident, happy girls and women.

Studies prove that the more powerful, successful, and happy a man becomes, the more people trust and like him, but the more powerful and happy a woman becomes, the fewer people trust her. With their brazen defiance and refusal to follow directions, girls who are bold enough to break those rules make us want to put them back into their cages.

That little girl on the soccer pitch could have quite easily been me.

Reading that book made the light bulb go off inside my head, the sudden realisation that it wasn't me, it was them. The pre-conditioning they had as children and through early adolescence made them dislike me and want to bully me. It wasn't anything I had done after all – hallelujah!!

I could finally understand why those kids at the tennis club behaved that way, why the girls in high school tried to attack me on the hockey pitch, why one of my friend's mums didn't want me to play with her daughter as she thought I was too ordinary, why people in my previous relationships had tried to control me and make me feel like I was nothing, why a senior team member of a competitor told me to "take my award and f@*k off" at an awards ceremony, why former colleagues had tried to shoot me down, belittle me, or worse still, act like I didn't exist, making decisions that affected my team behind my back and without consulting me.

That lightbulb moment I have transformed my life. I could finally be at peace with what had happened in my past, and I promised myself I would no longer allow it to affect my future. I would forgive my bullies and make it my mission that no one should be made to feel like that and should all have the confidence, self-belief, and courage they deserve.

I was no longer going to try and fit into someone else's box; I was going to stay in one that was purposefully built for me.

ONE: The Cause

When we think about confidence or lack thereof, we focus on dealing with the symptoms rather than the cause.

Focusing on the symptoms is like papering over the cracks or sticking plaster over an open wound.

No one is born lacking confidence; we all come into this world with a growth mindset and constantly fail while we learn to walk and talk. So, what changes?

Why do some people remain confident and maintain that growth mindset while others don't?

So, to understand the root cause as to why some people lack confidence and some people don't, I started with self-analysis, looking at my upbringing and my character.

I looked at what I witnessed through my own experience and my own family, what I'd experienced in the playground and finally researched through the books I'd read or the survey I undertook.

Self-Analysis

I have done much work on this, from profiling tools to DNA tests. I wanted to understand why I am so different to some of my friends, family, and co-workers.

Why do I now have an abundance of confidence in my ability to achieve something, yet my friends don't?

What makes me brave and willing to take on new challenges, but others doubt themselves?

What knocked my confidence and kept me from celebrating my achievements?

Why was it that whenever I achieved something great, like winning an award or getting a promotion, putting my head above the parapet, someone with a hammer was waiting to push me back down again, like a game of whack-a-mole?

Witnessed

I also drew analysis from the experiences I have witnessed through my upbringing and that of my family and friends.

When I talk about family, I refer to my immediate family; when I speak about my friends, it is those I have known for the best part of my life.

I have also witnessed the experiences in the playground with my daughter and her friends and how different parenting styles can affect children.

Research

And finally, research. Both through books I have read, including The Imposter Cure by Dr Jessamy Hibbert, You Are Enough by Cheryl Rickman, The Confidence Code, or the most enlightening for me, Untamed by Glennon Doyle and Wolfpack by Abby Wambach.

I recently commissioned my study, which backed up my original hunch. Further exploration needs to be done here, but I have a good enough baseline to know there is consistency and connected tissue.

When I combine self-analysis with witnessed experiences, books I have read, and research, conditioning is the common thread that keeps appearing repeatedly.

The conditioning we all had throughout our upbringing from parents, carers, teachers, early relationships, and other external influences has played a massive part in killing our confidence in adulthood.

We have become a product of our environment and the expectations that were put upon us. The characters we grew up with have all planted seeds that have grown over time and are now like deep-rooted oak trees, standing solid in our emotions.

Little seeds have become trees of emotions that include anxiety, self-doubt, fear of failure and untimely lead to us feeling like we are not good enough, brave enough or happy enough.

The good news is that the characters are unreal, just like any other book or film. They are just thoughts planted as seeds that, in turn, have turned into emotions.

After all, thoughts are not facts, and most of our thoughts are, in fact, thoughts.

TWO: Great Expectations

"Treat a man as he is, and he will remain as he is. Treat a man as he can and should be, and he will become as he can and should be" - Steven R Covey (Author of 7 Habits of Highly Effective People)

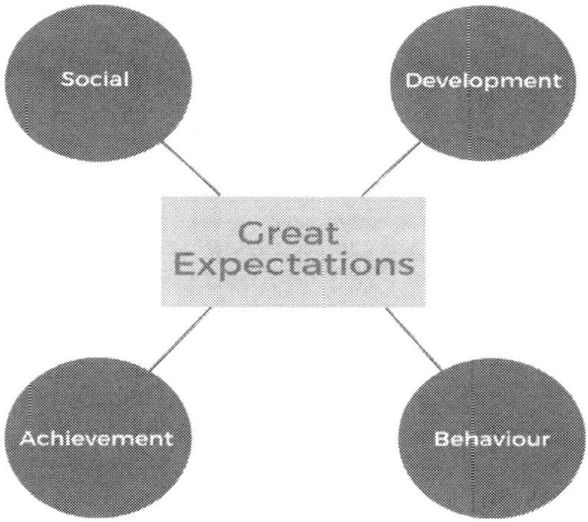

From the minute we are born, there is a level of expectation that is forced upon us by our parents, carers, teachers, and other influential people in our lives. You

become a data point that measures a world of averages and percentiles throughout childhood.
Expectations are set on how much you should weigh when you should start walking, talking, reading, and writing. Expectations on how you should behave, what you should look like and what you should achieve.

Should's left, right and centre, creating high, unrealistic expectations.

Social expectations and "shoulds" are placed around marriage, parenthood, and career success as we age.

Unfortunately, what you are expected to do often has very little to do with what you want and who you are.

Developmental Expectations

In the UK, from the minute you are born, your parents are given a little red book to measure your weight and height compared to other children your age. These developmental expectations carry on throughout your childhood.

Expectations on how quickly we learn to walk and talk, and then as you go into the school system, expectations are put upon you about when you learn to read and write.

Behavioural Expectations

In the same way, as expectations are put upon us around our development, expectations are also placed upon us on how we should behave from childhood.

Expectations of when you should speak and the volume you speak at. Expectations on how you should treat other people and your manners.

There are also different expectations depending on whether you're a boy or a girl. Your cultural background and social demographic also have a huge part to play.

Achievement Expectations

When you enter the education system, new expectations of what you should achieve come to life.

Expectations of your academic ability, with a strong focus on Maths, English, Science, History and Geography, start from the day you enter Reception to when you leave high school or further education.

Exams and tests are forced upon you throughout your education, constantly testing and comparing you with your peers.

Expectations to achieve specific grades in SATs, GCSEs, A 'Levels and then degrees. Depending on your cultural background, even greater expectations and added pressures on education can be placed upon you.

The pressure of expectations doesn't stop there.

Once you have finished your education, you are exposed to society's expectations.

Social Expectations

Social expectations are implicit rules that govern one's reactions and beliefs in a way society considers acceptable.

Social expectations depend not only on the individual but also on culture, religion, age group, class, and location and have skyrocketed since the birth of social media.

Social expectations carry on throughout your life, taking centre stage around the time when you leave education.

Expectations on who your partner will be and when you will learn to drive and buy your first car. The career you choose, how much money you earn and when you will rent or buy your first house. Then the expectations come around marriage, then children.

It's just never-ending.

Reflection Questions

Before moving on, take a moment to reflect on what expectations you have witnessed or experienced. Ask yourself the following questions and write down the responses.

- Which of these expectations have you experienced or witnessed?
- Which expectations have had the most significant impact on you or other people?

- How did these expectations make you or others feel?
- Which one expectation, if you changed it, would positively impact you or someone else?

Notes

THREE: Conditioning

"A child will never listen to a word you say, but they will imitate everything you do" - Angela Duckworth (Author of GRIT).

In addition to life's great expectations, we all receive a level of conditioning through certain characters we encounter throughout life.

We encounter these characters in the form of our parents, carers, teachers or early adulthood. You may have only met one of them, or you could have encountered all or only recognise parts.

These characters have influenced and shaped how much confidence we have going into adulthood. They have inadvertently planted the seeds of doubt, uncertainty, fear, anxiety, and stress.

The Characters of Conditioning

These characters carry negative traits and can have one or more essential characteristics. Introducing the Characters of Conditioning: The Perfectionist, The Professor, The Protector, The Comparer, The Critic and The Victim.

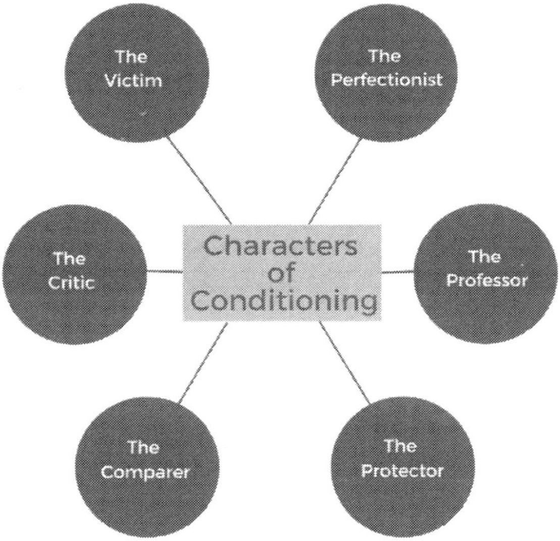

The Perfectionist

The Perfectionist is constantly striving for flawlessness and perfection.

I have encountered numerous perfectionists throughout my life, both male and female. Their constant striving for perfection and the pressure they put on themselves and sometimes others is relentless.

They believe they should be perfect in every way, including their appearance, work output, and behaviour.

According to the research conducted by Hewitt and Flett in 1991, there are three types of perfectionism, which in tune means three kinds of perfectionists:

1. **Self-orientated perfectionists** - hold themselves to incredibly strict (often unattainable) standards, avoid failure and are highly critical of themselves.

2. **Socially prescribed perfectionists** - feel pressured to be perfect based on other people's lofty expectations and excessive demands placed on them. This is the type of perfectionism that is most prevalent in modern-day society.

3. **Other-oriented perfectionists** - expect others to be perfect and judge people based on unrealistically high standards.

The other-oriented perfectionist most likely started life as self-orientated or socially prescribed, expecting the same as others.

The Professor

The Professor is a highly intelligent academic who is an expert in their field, finds learning easy and is top of their class and A Grade student.

Incredibly bright and a natural genius, they put a much higher value on IQ than EQ.

Facts, not emotions, are the order of the day; if they don't know it already, it's not worth knowing.

They have more accreditations and qualifications than most people have had hot dinners. They will most likely be seen in the library or applying for Mensa.

The Professor has incredibly high academic expectations of both them and others. They judge everyone based on their ability and can have a low opinion of anyone they feel doesn't match their intelligence.

They can often have a fixed mindset, believing that your intelligence is finite, something you are born with, and that can't change much apart from the areas of expertise.

If they don't find something easy, they will unlikely pursue it. It can be seen in any culture, but they are more prevalent in cultures where academic ability is regarded as the number one attribution to success.

The Protector

The Protector, also known as the Helicopter Parent, wraps their children and anyone else they have responsibility for in bubble wrap and cotton wool.

They hover over them, ensuring they are there to catch or pick them up the minute they fall. They are overconcerned with the smallest of injuries and can often have the local doctors on speed dial.

Never too far away, ready to pounce on any potential predator, they see danger at every possibility and are likely to have done a risk assessment of the school run.

The Protector is also likely to be overly anxious and highly concerned about their safety and that of their dependents. They constantly worry about what could go wrong rather than what could go right.

They are always reading the negative press, allowing it to influence their thoughts on the world and often hang around with other like-minded individuals, fuelling their anxiety and concerns.

The Comparer

The Comparer often evaluates themselves or their dependents about others. They want what other people have. They “envy up” or “scorn down" and compare everything and everyone.

The Comparer compares it all: academic ability, career, social status, wealth, or weight. The Comparer often flicks through social media and compares their life to others.

They are always looking out for the latest fad and love to be the first person to have purchased or tried it. Their constant comparisons can make them push themselves and their dependents to unattainable levels of excellence.

Unhealthily competitive, they want the biggest house, car and desirable wardrobe, hate themselves or their dependents losing to anyone, and often cheat to get what they want.

The Critic

The Critic holds a very high standard of themselves and others. They have their way of doing things and don't have any problem telling you what that is. They will happily criticise you for doing things your way.

The Critic can often be seen passing judgment on others and giving you their opinion whether you want it or not. They probably have a better way of doing things and don't hold back telling you what that is.

They always think they are correct and don't like to consider that there could be an alternative solution to a challenge. Set in their way of doing things and argumentative, they always want the last word and get defensive if you disagree.

The Victim

The Victim is the most negative of our characters and never takes ownership of their challenges and issues. The Victim has a fixed mindset, believes they are who they are and nothing can change them and always has someone else ready to blame.

The Victim is always ready with a list of excuses and reasons for not doing or achieving something. It's never their fault; it never has been and never will be. You will often find the victims walling in self-pity and feeling sorry for themselves.

Reflection Questions

Before moving on, take a moment to reflect on what conditioning you may have experienced or witnessed. Ask yourself the following questions and write down the responses.

- Which of these traits or characters have you experienced or witnessed?
- Which of these traits or characters can you see yourself?
- How do these characters or traits make you feel?
- Which of these characters or traits has had the most significant impact on your confidence?

Notes ____

FOUR: The Characters of Caution

"When a man gives his opinion, he's a man. When a woman gives her opinion, she's a bitch" - Bette Davis (American Actress)

In addition to the Characters of Conditioning, other characters could have impacted your confidence. These characters should be approached with caution or avoided altogether.

The Characters of caution may have appeared during your childhood, early adolescence, or career. They might have been your friends' parents, toxic partners in early relationships or power-hungry co-workers.

They have incredibly high expectations of others and believe everyone has a place and should stay in that place.

They put people in boxes, are incredibly judgmental and harness negative emotions such as jealousy and resentment.

They generate feelings of embarrassment, imposter syndrome and feelings of not being good enough to people who have fallen prey to their behaviours. Let's meet The Snob, The Misogynist, The Queen Bee and The Prince and Princess.

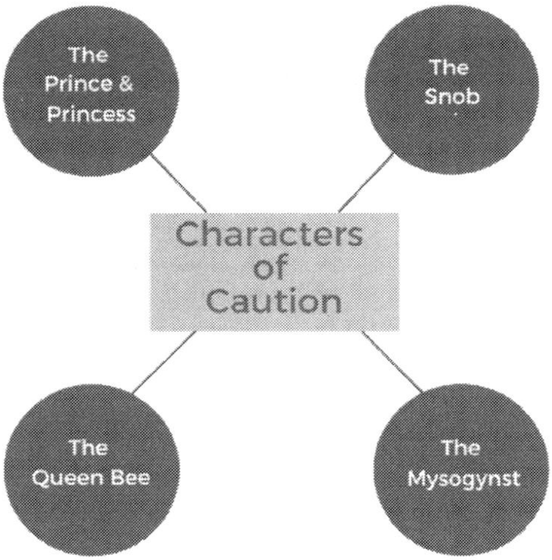

The Misogynist

The Misogynist can take on various forms and can be both male and female.

The male Misogynist believes that a woman's place should be at home and not in a successful career. Elitist and arrogant, they have an incredibly high opinion of themselves and an over-inflated ego.

They are intimidated by confident, strong women and struggle to accept them as equals.

The female Misogynist is just like the male. She also believes that women should be at home looking after the children, not aspiring to have careers and look down on any female who wants to be treated equally.

The Snob

Like the TV character Hyacinth Bucket, the Snob, the Stepford Wife or elitist characters who have been to Eton or Harvard, is someone with an exaggerated respect for high social position or wealth. They seek to associate with social superiors and look down on those regarded as socially inferior.

They like to think that they, along with their children, are better than everyone else and want to only associate with their type of people.

Like the Misogynist, the Snob is elitist and can often have afternoon tea in a twin set and pearls, play polo or hang out at the gentlemen's club. The Snob also has incredibly high expectations of their children to achieve and is highly competitive.

The Queen Bee

The Queen Bee wants to be powerful, can often think and behave like a man, and enjoys all the power for herself.

She thinks she is the only one deserving of her position, is superior to other women and kisses up and kicks down.

She is often manipulatively insincere, being nice to your face but bringing you down behind your back.

Most often found in the workplace or the school playground, they don't care where they show their power.

The Prince and Princess

Rarely impacting other people's confidence, the Prince and Princess are the least dangerous characters of caution unless they appear in your workplace or at school.

They live in a fantasy world where they believe they are far too unique or delicate to do any work.

They have been waited on hand and foot and are above doing anything they deem demining.

They have been made to believe they are extraordinary and expect to be treated as such. Most likely, the children of The Snob or The Misogynist.

Reflection Questions

Before moving on, take a moment to reflect on what Characters of Caution you may have experienced or witnessed. Ask yourself the following questions and write down the responses.

- Which of these characters have you experienced or witnessed?
- How do these characters make you feel?
- Which of these characters or traits have the most significant impact on your confidence?

Notes

FIVE: Time for Change

"Who was I before I became whom the world told me to be" - Glennon Doyle (Author of Untamed)

Living your life based on other people's high expectations and conditioning is holding you back from reaching your full potential and discovering who it was you were meant to be.

It creates unnecessary self-doubt, anxiety, fear of failure and a general sense that you are not good enough.

If you want to change your feelings, you must change your thoughts. You must unravel all those pre-conditioned pathways to negative emotions and create new ones in happier places.

You must dig deep into your past, unroot all the unrealistic expectations placed on you, and plant new seeds that allow you to grow into the person you were always meant to be.

Change is hard. It requires a tremendous amount of effort, which is why so many people stay as they are and are happy to blame everyone else for how they feel.

But that isn't you because otherwise, you wouldn't have started reading this book in the first place.

A World of Should's

"Should is an asshole!" - Jennifer Pastiloff (Author of On Being Human: A Memoir or Waking Up, Living Real, and Listening Hard)

As Jennifer politely quotes, should is an asshole. Living in a world of shoulds and great expectations is incredibly debilitating.

The only way you can move forward is to understand the facts and break down the associated myths.

Developmental Expectations

With constant comparisons to other children from the day you are born, it is no wonder they carry on throughout your life.

However, no two people on this planet are the same, not even identical twins. We are all unique and should be treated that way.

We all come into this world with different physicalities and abilities. Some people are short, others are tall, some are slim, and others are chubby. Some people have blue eyes and brown hair, while others have black hair and green eyes.

Some people are born with disabilities or are neurodiverse, yet we are expected to develop at the same rate. Genetics plays a huge role, and you can't decide on your genes.

Some people are naturally academic, others creative, yet the expectations put upon us are based on a minimal set of averages.

Appreciate yourself for who you are. Embrace your uniqueness and differences and that of those around you.

Behavioural Expectations

In addition to the expectations that are put upon you around the basics like manners and how you treat people, different expectations are placed upon you depending on whether you're a boy or a girl.

If you were born a boy, allowances are often made for your boisterous behaviour. You can be loud, raucous, aggressive, and even rude without anybody batting an eyelid.

Yet, if you were born a girl, there is an expectation for you to be polite, quiet, caring, considerate and kind, and you are rewarded for behaving that way.

However, because of these expectations put upon girls, they don't always stand up for what they believe in, ask for a pay rise, or put themselves forward for promotions, contributing to the gender pay gap and lack of women in the c-suite.

Boys are expected to be tough and not show emotions, always being told that boys don't cry and to 'man' up. However, these expectations of not showing emotions and being able to say how you feel cause mental illnesses

like depression and severe anxiety. This can lead to self-harm or, worse still, suicide.
According to an article written in March 2020 by the Royal College of Paediatrics and Child Health (RCPCH), between the ages of 15-24 in the UK, male suicides were three times more common than female suicides (ONS total of 532 total male suicides, compared to 182 total female suicides in 2018).

However, your behaviour should not be defined by whether you are born a boy or a girl, your culture or social demographic.

Your behaviour should align with your values, morals, and principles. If something doesn't align, you should be confident to speak up and disagree.

If you are a female, you should be able to ask for a pay rise or a promotion; if you are male, talk about your feelings and emotions. It doesn't make you weak. It will make you stronger.

Achievement Expectations

While the way we are taught has evolved with the introduction of technology, the curriculum hasn't evolved much since the early 20th century.

The focus remains on numeracy, literacy, and academic ability rather than other skills and abilities, such as creativity or emotional intelligence.

Like the curriculum, the expectation of ability hasn't progressed as far as it could have to accommodate people's individual needs and capabilities. Similarly, with developmental expectations, the data only looks at averages and assumes everyone is the same.

However, we know that everyone is different and has their own needs, and the education system hasn't caught up. It doesn't consider learning difficulties such as dyslexia or the challenges that neurodiverse children with ADHD or Autism have.

Whilst most schools will do their best with the available funding and support, there still needs to be more money or resources in the state education systems to cater to these needs. This leaves people feeling like they have failed and must strive to reach the expected attainments.

The expectations of achievement from different cultures and ethnic minorities are also outdated. The additional pressures they face stem from first-generation immigrants from developing countries who migrated to the West.

To benefit from all the West had to offer, migrants who were educated and had achieved professional qualifications, such as MBAs, PhDs and BSCs in subjects such as Maths, Engineering and Medicine, went on to have desirable careers in the West. Yet individuals who were less educated could only expect to have manual jobs, such as cleaners and factory workers.

Therefore, because of what they had to do to be successful and have fulfilling careers, they apply the same pressures to achieve in 2nd, the 3rd, 4th and even 5th generations, even though they no longer need these careers to succeed. Multiple studies show that education and academic ability have little impact on how successful or happy someone will be.

What you achieve is, therefore, unique to you and you only, to your abilities, passions, and values and not how well you did at school, college, or university.

In her book ‘Grit’, Angela Duckworth puts success down to passion and perseverance, not academic ability. So, rather than focusing on your grades, focus on discovering your true desires and building resilience.

Social Expectations

Social expectations are put upon you from the minute you are born and carry on throughout your life. Social expectations on how you behave, who your friends are and how happy you are.

Social expectations around who your partner will be and when you will learn to drive and buy your first car. The career you choose, how much money you earn and when you will rent or buy your first house. Then the expectations start to come around marriage, then children. They appear to be relentless.

However, most social expectations are generational or cultural and hugely outdated. Most of the generational expectations haven't moved on since the era of Queen

Victoria, especially around marriage and when you have children. Fortunately, we live in the 21st century, in a time of constant change and advancements in attitudes.

It would be best to avoid allowing these expectations to impact how you want to live. If you're going to stay single, stay single. If you want to buy a house and live with a partner before marriage, you should do it.

If you want to be a poet rather than a doctor, be a poet. If you want to have children, have them. If you don't, then don't feel pressured to do so.

Realistic Expectations

Embrace your flaws and uniqueness, behave how you see fit and in line with your values, celebrate your achievements no matter how big or small and live your own life how you want to.

And just like someone once told me, don't let someone else hold the pen that writes your future.

Confidence Creator: Write down all the unrealistic expectations that have been placed upon you and make new realistic, achievable goals aligned with your values. Write down all the fantastic things you have achieved and celebrate them individually.

Notes ____________________________________

SIX: Un-Conditioning

"If you don't like something, change it; if you can't change it, change your attitude towards it" - Maya Angelou (Poet and Author of Why the Caged Bird Sings)

Hopefully, having debunked the myths of great expectations, it's time to do the same for the Characters of Conditioning and Caution.

The good news is, just like any other good book or film, the Characters of Conditioning and Caution are not real. They are just thoughts planted as seeds that have turned into negative emotions.

The average person has 50,000 -70,000 thoughts a day, and according to Dr Russ Harris, author of The Happiness Trap, 80 per cent of everyone's thoughts contain some harmful content.

Thankfully, thoughts are just that; they are rarely ever facts.

Before becoming the person you were always meant to be, you must un-condition your deep-routed pathways to these negative emotions and create new positive ones.

To help you do this, we need to look at the Characters and de-bunk the myths they have created as part of your conditioning and high expectations.

It's also worth noting that the Characters of Conditioning and Caution have not intentionally planted these seeds. These traits have been passed down from generation to generation, becoming a vicious circle.

Until now, that it is.

The Perfectionist

According to Jamil Qureshi's book, The Mind Coach, "Success is not a finite and tangible destination. It is a long and undulating journey. We are born imperfect, and we die that way. Therefore, we are always in a state of learning." Perfection is an unattainable level of expectation because there is always room for improvement.

People who constantly strive for perfection put off trying anything new for fear of failure or not being good enough. It's incredibly exhausting as you often work twice as hard to achieve something impossible.

It would be a shame for you not to reach your full potential because of the pressures of perfection put upon you by either yourself, other people or, worse still, what you expect from them.

Perfection is the Paralysis of Performance

If you recognise this trait in yourself and feel that the perfectionism you are applying to yourself and that of others is stopping you from achieving your goals, instead of trying to be perfect, embrace your imperfections and aim for levels of “good enough”.

Think of something that you have been procrastinating on or haven’t yet completed because it's not perfect, and commit to start working on it again straight away. Start small and with version one. Focusing on version 10 is not going to get you anywhere. Remember, there is always room for improvement and good enough is much better than not done at all.

If you recognise this trait in someone else and it is holding you back from achieving your goals, forgive them for just trying to be perfect. It’s all they have known, after all.

Confidence Creator: Write down something you have been putting off and commit to getting started. Write down when you are going to have this completed.

Notes ______________________________________

The Professor

Not all of us are born a natural genius, and that's OK for those who aren't. Intelligence comes in various forms, and EQ is as equally important as IQ. You don't need a piece of paper to prove your capability. After all, you can't get a degree in empathy or creativity.

Experience and life skills are more important than academic ability for some careers and roles. In her book Grit, Angela Duckworth states that Americans endorse “being hard-working” nearly five times as often as they endorse “intelligence”. She also says that her research proves that passion and resilience are the keys to success, not academic ability or intelligence.

You Are a Genius

Suppose you recognise this trait in yourself, and the professor is making you judge yourself and others by how many accreditations you hold or your IQ. Learn to appreciate that intelligence comes in various forms and is not the marker for success.

Stop focusing on the things you or they are not great at and focus on yours and their extraordinary strengths. Work together to identify the skills they have that are different to yours and celebrate those skills.

If you recognise this trait in someone else and it is holding you back from achieving your goals, forgive them as they have been fortunate to find learning easy, have a natural gift for learning, and keep focusing on your extraordinary strengths.

Confidence Creator: Write down all the fantastic skills you have learnt and all your talents and celebrate them.

Notes

The Protector

Being protective and concerned for people's safety is part of our auto responses that were formed to keep us alive in the Stone Age, and awareness of danger is a good thing if it is associated with potential death. Thankfully, most risks we face today do not result in death, at worst, a trip to the doctor or hospital.

Whilst your intentions may be good, being overly protective can cause anxiety and stress to yourself and the people you encounter. I have witnessed first-hand how the over-protectiveness of a parent unduly caused fear and doubt in my child, who is, until this time, incredibly confident in her ability.

Just spending too much time listening to their concerns and stories of what could go wrong or had gone wrong in the past led my daughter not to be able to sleep at night or fear a particular horse at a riding lesson.

You cannot be protected from everything; there will be times when you must stand on your own two feet and face your fears. Fear of failure is one of the biggest things that will hold you back from gaining confidence.

In everything we have done in life, we have failed at first, and to fail is only the "**F**irst **A**ttempt **i**n **L**earning". Remember that fear stands for **F**alse **E**vidence **A**ppearing **R**eal. It's an emotion based on how we think about something, so learn to face your fears and start failing.

If you recognise this trait in yourself, being protective and concerned for people's safety generally comes from a good place, so firstly, understand it's an instinct that has grown over time. However, this trait also keeps you and those around you from achieving your full potential.

Think about something you have been too scared to try and write down the reasons stopping you. You will soon realise that all those reasons are thoughts and not facts, so there should be no stopping you from going ahead and doing it.

If you have dependents, you must show them how to be brave, not just tell them. You can't tell your child not to fear spiders and then jump and scream the minute you see one. As Angela Duckworth says in her book Grit, "Children will not listen to a word you say, but they will imitate everything you do".

If you recognise this trait in someone else and it creates anxiety and stress and makes you fearful of trying new things, then understand that they are only trying to keep you alive and are concerned for your safety.

Cut yourself from those feelings by trying something you have been putting off due to fear.

Confidence Creator: Write down all those fears; you will soon realise they are thoughts, not facts. They are their fears, not yours. Do not allow what someone else fears to hold you back from achieving great things. Be brave. You know you want to.

Notes

The Comparer

According to an article written by Angela in Feb 2021 for Mind Body & Soul, comparisons are a natural human tendency and aren't inherently wrong. We do it all the time: we compare our current situation with where we came from, we compare our present self with our former self, we compare ourselves with others in our age group, and we compare our knowledge and abilities with others in our field. All of these are good things.

However, comparisons can be a double-edged sword. They can be a powerful motivator, but sometimes, they can be a strong deterrent from doing something. They can also be damaging to our mental health in the long term.

Comparisons are a normal part of human cognition and can be suitable for self-improvement. When we compare ourselves to others, we get information about what we want and where we want to be and provide valuable feedback on measuring up. However, they can also cause us much psychological pain. When we start comparing ourselves to others too much, we run into problems.

You Are Unique

If you find yourself using unhealthy comparisons to others, like Social Comparison, be mindful of both sides and know that everyone has different life experiences and luck.

You are the only person you should ever compare yourself to. We are all unique; no person is the same, not even identical twins. We all have our own fantastic set of capabilities and abilities that we are born with.

Confidence Creator: Write down everything you are excellent at and focus your efforts on being the best version of yourself.

Notes

The Critic

While some criticism leads to improvement and development, others can harm one's self-esteem.

Criticism can be constructive or negative, depending on the critic's intention, how it is presented, and how the person being criticised perceives it.

Negative criticism is usually delivered from a place of jealousy, spite, or anger, and it can focus on the apparent flaw or error without offering suggestions on how to improve or correct the fault. Knowing what is wrong only sometimes implies knowing what is right.

Constructive Criticism, on the other hand, usually comes from a place of love and concern for the person or situation being criticised; on most occasions, the critic has a suggestion or correction to improve the person or situation. However, even constructive criticism can leave a person feeling inadequate and not good enough.

Encourage and Guide

We all have an unconscious bias and our way of doing things, but that doesn't mean it's the best way. You can reach the same destination by taking multiple different routes, but you always let the other person decide how they get there themselves.

You may like to get there quickly, and they may want to take the scenic route, but the destination is essential and different from “the way”.

Focus on the desired results; that's what's important. Give guidelines and resources, but let them choose their path.

Confidence Creator: Write down a job that needs doing and delegate it to someone. Give them guidance and support, but allow them to complete the task their way.

Notes

The Victim

People with a victim mentality feel bad things keep happening and the world is against them. They think everyone else is against them, whether their partner, co-workers, or even their family or friends. Even though there might be things that you can do to help fix the situation, they don't take responsibility for anything and feel as though everything is out of their control.

In addition, the victim might take things personally, even when they are not directed at them. Victims most likely went through a wrong time in their lives or experienced trauma but had no coping strategies and developed this opposing viewpoint or victim mindset.

It's easy to blame everyone else for your lot in life because that justifies feeling sorry for yourself. If it's never your fault, you don't have to do anything about it, and you can explain why you have not achieved your full potential.

Some people enjoy playing the Victim and wallowing in self-pity, but you can change if you choose to.

You Will Survive

Take ownership of your problems, focus on the things within your control and start taking positive steps towards improving them.

It takes effort, but you can change from a fixed, victim mindset to a growth one. Should you want to, that is.

Confidence Creator: Write down a challenge or issue you are facing that you have been making excuses or blaming someone else for. Rather than blame everyone else, take control of the problem and take back responsibility for finding a solution. Be the master of your destiny.

Notes

The Misogynist

Unfortunately, I have had the displeasure of encountering both the male and the female misogynist during my early adolescence and throughout my career.

According to an article published by Dr Prem Jagyasi, an Author and Speaker, on DrPrem.com. If you know a person who is undervaluing the value of someone just because she happens to be a female, then you are indeed dealing with a misogynist. You do not have to be necessarily a man to be a misogynist; you could very well be a woman.

Misogyny can be even more harmful when it springs for women, as they get away with it more quickly. The worst thing is, you can't even get away from them. They are everywhere. They are at school, your workplace and sometimes even your home.

Misogynists are generally easy to recognise because their behaviour towards women may be disturbing or annoying. They are full of contempt and envy women who win over them or belittle a female's accomplishments. Sometimes, they may be nice to you in public but cut you out in private. So, if someone around you or someone close to you is a misogynist, you might feel irritated and intimidated.

Returning to the cavemen and women, we need each other for survival. Whether that is taking on the roles of hunter and gatherer or keeping the gene pool alive by having children. We have complementary skills and talents and have every right to have successful careers and be treated as equals. We should be able to celebrate our achievements and accomplishments and demand what we deserve.

Philogyny Not Misogyny

According to Dr Prem, men are generally misogynists because they were raised in a patriarchal society or within dysfunctional families. Most misogynists had poor relationships with their mothers or have experienced bad relationships. This makes them overly critical of all women.

They may feel like they are the ones who must provide and be the breadwinner, while the women should be at home looking after the children and doing the household chores. Communicating your thoughts is the best way to deal with a misogynist.

For instance, if you think a misogynist constantly belittles you at work, you must talk to them about it. You do have the option to tell them how their behaviour makes you feel.

Confidence Creator: Write down how they make you feel and make a point to tell them. Ensure you don't say it harshly; the point here is not to oppress. Use light words and measure your sentences so you don't invite useless arguments. Be calm. This will help you deliver your point. If your discussion becomes an argument, leave the topic alone and either talk about something else or make an excuse and leave. Although this might make a misogynist feel they have won, there is no point in sitting and arguing. The same goes for any partner who is a misogynist.

Notes

The Queen Bee

Like the Misogynists, I have encountered numerous Queen Bees, both personally and professionally. It's mainly women who have negatively impacted my career and confidence.

According to an article written in March 2013 by John Baldoni in Forbes, the term "queen bee syndrome" comes from work done by University of Michigan researchers in the 1970s on the issue of female bosses. According to their work published in Psychology Today in 1974, these women operating in male hierarchies sought to preserve their rare turf by thwarting other women's attempts to rise as they had done. Sadly, as Drexler argues, such bias still exists.

Research that Drexler cites shows that women bosses can also be bullies. According to a 2010 study by the Workplace Bullying Institute, "female bullies directed their hostilities toward other women 80% of the time – up 9% since 2007."

By contrast, male bullies aimed their abuse at both genders. In a 2011 study of 1,000 working women by the American Management Association, 95% felt they had been "undermined by another woman at some point in their careers."

Thinking you are the "best thing since sliced bread" and better than everyone else is a very lonely place. Ever watchful for someone, ready to take their place as top dog or bring them down to lower levels, must also be very exhausting. Imagine a life where you cannot trust anyone for fear of them working out who you are.

And as Kim Scott says in her book Radical Candor, "There is a special place in hell for people who kiss up and kick down".

Take Out the Sting

Queen bees may be around us, but that does not mean the people they have authority over do not have options. Stand up for what you think is right demonstrates courage and savvy. These are just the kind of attributes that organisations need in positions of leadership. If you encounter a Queen Bee, how do you neutralise their behaviour and not be victimised?

According to an article written in September 2018 by Mandy Garner of Working Mums, you must be proactive and create options for yourself. Develop Yourself: Sign up for training courses to improve your industry knowledge and skillset. Expand Your Network: Join professional networks at your company and within your industry. Find Sponsors: Develop strong professional relationships with senior decision-makers in your organisation that can influence your career.

Explore New Career Opportunities: You don't have to stay in a toxic work environment. Get out there, speak to headhunters, get interviews, and see what other opportunities are available.

Make strong alliances within your industry so you have some support. Do Not React When Provoked: Queen Bees love to push your buttons and get a reaction. Remain calm. Do not show emotion. Always be polite and do not engage in gossip or petty talk. Use your energy to develop yourself and expand your network.

And if you've spotted worrying signs of Queen Bee Syndrome in yourself, look at the causes of your insecurity; these will only hold you back in the long run.

Confidence Creator: Write down the best course of action you will take based on your situation. Act on making it happen today.

Notes

The Snob

Snobbery is an unattractive trait caused by a person's belief that they are inherently better than others. Most snobbery concerns social class and the idea that someone who has more money or went to a fancier school is more worthy than someone who doesn't have these advantages.

Whether it's through wearing brand-name labels, pouring drinks from the most prized wine bottles, or just putting on the presumed airs and graces of the upper class, people who engage in snobbery can make us doubt our self-worth.

Maintaining such high expectations of others and themselves must be incredibly exhausting. The constant comparison and addiction to social status and social media mean they can never let their guard down. Money and status don't buy happiness, but that doesn't stop them from trying to show the world it does.

Be Inclusive

According to Susan Krauss Whitbourne, PhD, ABPP article published in October 2014, in Psychology Today, snobs find it essential to distinguish themselves from others. For their snobbery to work, though, they need their target to self-identify as inferior: You can't be a snob in a vacuum. There always must be another group of people who feel it's justified for someone else to define them as inferior.

Confidence Creator: Don't buy into their behaviour and rise above it. Think about where their behaviour came from and forgive them. Take pride in what makes you unique, and continue to be grateful for everything you have.

Notes ____

The Prince and Princess

Princess syndrome usually refers to a noticeable form of narcissism in women. Although the metaphor relates to women, it is also a common symptom seen in men and is referred to as Prince Syndrome. People with such syndrome are characterised by an arrogant/self-centred/attention-seeking/demanding attitude. They live like a fairy tale, always cherry-picking the pretty/beautiful things and complaining/frowning at the odd ones.

They may think they are unique when they are often spoilt, overindulged and very needy. They depend on others to make them feel good and struggle to survive in the real world.

Kiss the Frog

A recent tweet by Adam Grant, an organisational psychologist and best-selling author, suggests that telling kids they're superior doesn't build self-esteem. It breeds narcissism. Research suggests narcissists don't suffer from a lack of love.

They're the product of parents with inflated views of them. Healthy parenting says, "You're special to me," not "you deserve special treatment".

Confidence Creator: If you see this trait in yourself, firstly try to understand how you came to be this way; it could most likely be a result of how your parents made you feel. We all want the best for our children, but creating unrealistic and unattainable expectations can have severe repercussions in the real world.

Notes

SEVEN: Re-Conditioning

"Confidence is the purity of action with a mind free of doubt" – Katy Kay & Claire Shipman (Authors of The Confidence Code).

To move forward and become the person you truly want to be, you must re-condition your thoughts and choose different characters. Characters help you create positive emotions and help you become the person you were meant to be.

These characters will help you create new positive pathways and traits. You can create as many positive traits as possible and take on as many characters as possible.

Introducing the Characters of Confidence, The Warrior, The Leader, The Competitor, The Cheerleader, The Inspector and The Coach.

The
Coach
The
Warrior
The
Inspector
Characters
of
Confidence
The
Leader
The
Cheerleader
The
Competitor

The Warrior

Fiercely independent, The Warrior believes they can achieve anything they want. They are courageous and throw themselves into any challenge, big or small.

They fight for what they believe in and stand up for anyone they believe to be poorly treated. If someone says it can't be done, the Warrior proves it can.

Solutions and not problems are the order of the day, and they will go out of their way to help anyone in need.

Embrace Your Inner Warrior

To help nurture your inner warrior, pick a challenge you have been putting off for fear of failure and commit to starting it immediately. Get out of your comfort zone, smash through the fear zone, and feel the benefits of entering the learning and growth zones.

Allow setbacks to build resilience. If you fall, dust yourself off and get straight back up again. Learn from your mistakes and keep pushing forward. Be bold and brave. The Warrior can achieve anything they want.

Confidence Creator: Write down a challenge you have been putting off and set a date of when you will have completed it.

Notes

Yvonne Matzk

The Leader

The Leader is experienced and knowledgeable and guides others along the way. An inspirational role model the Leader practises what they preach and leads from the front and by example.

Do as I do, not just do as I say; the Leader encourages and supports the next generation by passing on their knowledge and skills. The Leader sees everyone as an equal and treats everyone with respect.

As the famous saying goes, give a man a fish, he will eat for a day; teach them to fish, and they will eat every day.

Leaders don't give people the fish. Leaders teach them how to do it.

Lead by Example

Embrace your inner leader by demonstrating how something should be done. Show others the way rather than just telling someone how to do something. Please don't just give them the solution. Teach and guide them how to get there themselves.

Allow them to make mistakes and learn how to fail. After all, to fail is just the "first attempt in learning".

Confidence Creator: Write down the name of someone who has asked for your support or advice on how to do something and commit to helping them.

Notes

The Competitor

The Competitor is highly competitive and gives everything they do 110%.

They try their best and are always looking for ways to improve either themselves or others around them.

Driven by goals and targets, the Competitor always strives to beat their last performance.

Whilst incredibly competitive, they lose gracefully and see it as an opportunity to learn and do better next time.

Start the Race

Embrace your inner competitor, think of something you want to improve, and set a target of how and when you will achieve it. Break it into achievable, bite-size chunks and keep track of your progress.

Keep moving forward, adjusting as and when needed along the way. Have a competition with yourself and go for gold.

Confidence Creator: Write down a goal you want to achieve but have not started. Break it down and set yourself realistic targets and milestones.

Notes

The Cheerleader

The Cheerleader is happy for others to take the lead, is an excellent team player and always encourages and supports their team members.

The Cheerleader is satisfied in their skin, grateful for what they have and wants others to be as fulfilled as they are.

Nurturing and empathetic, the Cheerleader makes sure everyone is included and feels valued and treated fairly.

Grab Your Pompoms

Just like the captains of cheer squads, the cheerleaders are known for perpetuating team spirit. They support others, encourage participation, and are the first to clap for others' achievements.

Cheerleaders know how to motivate and inspire in an uplifting way. They commit to the success of each team member by modelling qualities such as fairness, honesty, and commitment.

Encouraging others can have a lasting impact on them, but it takes practice. We all have what it takes to energise and empower our people; consistent cheering is contagious.

Confidence Creator: Celebrate big and small wins with your friends, family, and co-workers. Commit to recognising others' achievements and watch as those around you are inspired to act similarly while building trust and respect. So, grab your pompoms and show others how it's done.

Notes

The Inspector

The Inspector looks for the facts and the proof of the situation. They write down everything and ensure there is supporting evidence before acting upon it.

The Inspector notes all your thoughts and takes them to court before giving a final verdict and deciding if they are innocent or guilty as charged.

They take the emotion out of every situation and look at everything through the lens of a logical and rational mind.

Get Out the Magnifying Glass

Most of what we think is happening is just a thought and not the reality of the situation. How many times have you had to apologise for reacting to a problem only to find out that it wasn't what happened?

Confidence Creator: Think on paper! Write everything down before you react or respond to a trigger or situation. Writing everything down will allow you to take the emotion out of any case and look for the facts.

Notes

The Coach

The Coach makes you see things for what they are and helps you compartmentalise facts over emotions. The cheerful voice inside your head checks the conditioned characters and works with you to create new pathways.

New auto-responses to the things that trigger our negative emotions. They focus on your strengths and natural ability and help you stay on track to reach your full potential.

They know that improvement requires effort, and they are with you every step of the way.

Shift Your Mindset

Embrace your inner coach by questioning your initial beliefs, allowing time to understand if your thoughts and feelings are based on emotion or logic.

Create a motivational voice to encourage, support and keep you on track. Allow your inner coach to focus on your strengths and work with you to improve where necessary.

Confidence Creator: Hold yourself accountable and make commitments and promises that keep moving you forward and achieving your goals. Make sure you write them down.

Notes

EIGHT: You Are Not Alone

Change is hard, but it is necessary to keep improving. To help you on your journey to greater confidence, you can do other things to help support you.

These include finding your superpower and your tribe, along with further reading.

Finding Your Superpower

We all have superpowers, unique abilities and character strengths that separate us from the next person, but how do we determine what they are?

There are various ways you can do this. One way is to ask other people what they think your unique abilities are: The skills and behaviour you find so easy and natural, yet others struggle to do. Your superpowers and unique abilities generally come so naturally to you that you think they're easy. Yet, others couldn't do them if they tried. You can email friends and family and ask them to tell you what they think your superpowers are and compare any consistencies.

Or, a quicker and easier option is to complete a series of profiling tools, like the VIA Character Survey (**www.viacharacter.org**). This tool is free and tells you your top five Character strengths. They also do a version for children, which is a fun activity to do with your kids.

According to the book Unique Ability 2.0, we are all born with a natural ability that is unique to us. Using the Kolbe A Index, you can discover what that is. The Kolbe A Index (Instinct Test) is excellent.

It does not measure intelligence, personality, or social style. It measures the intuitive ways you act when you strive. Use your custom Kolbe A Index Results to be more productive, less stressed, and unlock joy at work or with your family.

Another useful profiling tool is the Clifton Strengths Finder. The Clifton Strengths assessment gives you a personalised report that measures your talents and natural thinking patterns, feelings, and behaviours. The Kolbe and the Gallops are paid-for tools, but it is worth the investment if you find those things as fascinating as mine.

Finding Your Tribe

We were never meant to do this alone, so finding your tribe of like-minded people who support, inspire, encourage, and motivate you throughout your life and career can also have a massive positive impact on your confidence and self-belief.

You can have different tribes for the other areas of your life: a friendship tribe, a family tribe, and a work tribe.

I am incredibly privileged to have a fantastic tribe across all areas of my life, who have all been part of my journey to confidence and a family who motivates and inspires me daily.

Books

As well as the profiling tools, several books I have read helped me better understand confidence, mindset and the power of thought. These books include:

- The Confidence Code by Katy Kay and Claire Shipman
- Imposter Cure by Dr Jessamy Hibberd
- Mindset by Carol Dweck
- The Mind Coach by Jamil Qureshi
- Untamed by Glennon Doyle

- Wolfpack by Abby Wambach
- You Are Enough by Cheryl Rickman
- You Can't Hurt Me by David Goggins
- The Chimp Paradox by Prof Steve Peters

Reflection Questions

Take a moment to reflect on your superpowers and who you can enlist to support you on your journey. Ask yourself the following questions and write down the responses.

- What are your superpowers, and how will you use them in the future?
- Who is in your tribe that you can call upon for support and advice?
- Which books are you going to read or listen to gain further knowledge?
- What does the future look and feel like, and what steps will you take to ensure you get there?

Notes

NINE: Putting it All Together

Hopefully, by now, you have gained a better understanding of the impact that the great expectations and conditioning placed upon you growing up and recognised how your parents, teachers, carers, and environment have all contributed to your confidence.

This greater understanding should enable you to forgive the characters of conditioning and caution and begin to take on newly improved feelings and thoughts. Remember your superpowers, lean on your tribe, and commit to further reading to support you.

To help keep you on track and avoid falling prey to old habits and thoughts, it's time to take the pledge.

The Pledge

Repeat after me?

"I solemnly declare that I will no longer allow the expectations and conditioning of my past to affect my confidence in the future.

I also promise to stop forcing my conditioning onto others, allowing them to be who they are truly meant to be, which is the best version of themselves."

Hallelujah!

Taking Back the Pen

It's time to finally take back the pen and start writing your new future—forgiveness, knowledge, and, ultimately, more confidence. Good Luck!

Acknowledgements

As I mentioned earlier in my book, I am incredibly privileged to have a fantastic tribe of wonderful friends and family who have all been very supportive and encouraging throughout my life, career and writing this book.

However, I want to pay a special thank you to Julia Elliott, Melanie Kirkpatrick, Jacquie Rives, Emma Roberts, Vanessa Rees, Collette McGannon, Lindsey Betts, Anna Blake, Jade Wilson, Aggrey Lutta, Mark Collins, Leanne Benjamin, Colin Williams, Jamil Qureshi, Natalie Hailey and Hayley Roberts for all taking the time to read my first draft and provide honest and open feedback. Thank you also goes to everyone who took the time to complete the survey.

Extra special thanks also go to Olivia Jaskolka for being the first person to read, proofread and edit the first draft for me; I don't know what I would have done without you.

I also want to thank Jen and Tony (my Mum and Dad) and Michele and Gerry (my brother and sister) for not putting any expectations or conditioning on me.

About the Author

Yvonne is an author, speaker and coach with a successful sales and leadership career in the technology industry for over 25 years. Starting life in sales, Yvonne went on to lead a multi-million-pound division at CDW and was instrumental in winning multiple global awards.

On this journey, she became distinctly aware of the lack of females in both Sales, Technical and Executive roles, so she decided to help change that by supporting Women in Technology. Yvonne does this by delivering keynotes, hosting, or participating in panels and mentoring.

Yvonne has been a member of numerous Partner Advisory Boards with her most recent IDC and is a champion of initiatives helping young women into IT.

Yvonne is also a judge for the CRN Women in Channel Awards CRN Channel Awards and is featured on CRN's A-List.

Now a Worldwide Association of Business Coaches™ (WABC™), Registered Corporate Coach™ (RCC™), ILM Accredited Business Coach, Leading Energy Profile Practitioner and motivated by making a difference, Yvonne founded Coachere.

Combining her vast experience with Coaching, Yvonne now helps organisations work more effectively through better communication and collaboration and for individuals to gain the confidence they need for success.

Yvonne also recently founded The Channel Community, along with several industry friends. The Channel Community was created to connect like-minded people across the IT Channel to help individuals reach their full potential through Mentoring.

Yvonne is a devoted mother to Alexia, happily married to Rob, and, in her spare time, enjoys running, playing tennis (still), travelling, and spending time with family and friends. **www.yvonnematzk.com**

About Coachere

Coachere works to increase the self-awareness, resilience, confidence, and performance of professionals in sales, solutions, partner management and exec leadership positions within the IT channel and adjacent industries.

We combine over 25 years of experience in sales, partner management, and executive leadership positions in the IT channel with various coaching techniques and methods, either by purpose-built workshops or one-to-one or group coaching and mentoring.

Passionate about people, partnerships, and a global award-winning track record, Coachere can also help organisations build meaningful relationships, profitable go-to-market strategies and vital partner ecosystems in the IT channel through consulting. **www.coachere.com**

About The Channel Community

The Channel Community was created to connect like-minded people across the Channel who want to help support individuals reach their full potential through Mentoring. The community has also been created to support and advise on Channel-specific issues. **www.thechannelcommunity.com**

Printed in Poland
by Amazon Fulfillment
Poland Sp. z o.o., Wrocław
08 November 2023

e6f32e1f-86dd-4ea6-8b39-79a5b210db83R01